DR. PAUL'S 99¢ CURES

WORRY & ANXIETY

DR. PAUL J. YOUNG

Dr. Paul's 99¢ Cures

Worry & Anxiety

Dr. Paul J. Young

A
TOTAL RELIEF SYSTEMS publication

DrPaulYoung.com

INTRODUCTION

99¢ CURE...REALLY?

____

SO YOU ARE **WORRIED** AND FULL OF ANXIETY. YOU MAY BE STRUGGLING WITH THESE ANXIETIES:

1. You are afraid of driving and getting into an accident
2. You have difficulty concentrating
3. You feel agitated and restless
4. You are anxious about raising your children and all the difficulties they and you face in the future
5. You are anxious whether you are REALLY LOVED by your husband/wife/children/anyone else
6. You worry about driving with another person lest they make a mistake and you get injured
7. Worried about your debt
8. You fear running out of money now and in retirement
9. You find it hard to concentrate
10. If you are older, you worry about failing
11. You don't want to look stupid

12. You don't like to be alone
13. You are irritable too many times
14. You have trouble falling asleep or staying asleep
15. You are anxious about job security
16. You worry about your health
17. You are tense, muscle tight
18. Anxious about getting old
19. You are anxious about your relationships
20. Anxious about how you look
21. Worry about your weight
22. Worried about your safety or the safety of your family and those you love
23. Anxious about being late for work, a plane or appointment
24. You worry and are anxious about your past and what you man have done
25. You avoid social situations
26. You may worry about your eduction, future work and career
27. You are anxious about the pressures of work, family and expectations of others that you find hard to fulfill.

Worry. Anxiety. You struggle with it too much.

That's why you bought this book, hoping for a cure…for 99¢ (more if your bought the paperback). And you smiled when you paid less than a dollar for some help that you would pay a thousand dollars for, maybe a lot more.

It is true, you may have spent thousands on therapy and pills…and are still suffering from anxiety.

What could a book like this do for you?

You laugh.

Kind of stupid, isn't it, believing that I could help you when no one else has?

Or is it?

Maybe I know something that you don't know, something that will take you deep inside your inner self, shine a light on it and help you to fix it.

What if?

So you wonder if I can really fix you…for good, or whether you will keep searching for some lost formula, some hidden elixir that will make everything right again.

Yep, a 99¢ cure.

Frankly, it's not a 99¢ cure. It cost me years of study - over seven years of academic study after college, all the time, the tens of thousands of dollars I spent to learn what I know, as well as all the decades of experience.

This is no 99¢ cure - at least for me.

Yet you get in on what I know, all the years of experience helping people around the world, thousands of people, one on one, in small groups and in crowds sometimes larger than a thousand, as I taught people principles about life and how to find happiness, peace and joy and help you to get over the anxiety you feel.

Today, a great host of people have experienced deep changes in their lives because I shared with them what I believe to be the awesome secret to a happy, peaceful and joy filled life.

And I want to share it with you, all for only for little!
Quite a deal, isn't it?

I trade all I have learned, all the lessons I have taught people about how to break through one's anxiety, all the steps that are so often lost and never talked about in most therapist's sessions.

All of it, all of me for only 99¢.

It's a steal!

But not if you stop reading. You need to follow me all the way through this short but powerful read.

Why will it be powerful, the kind of power that could make a difference in your life?

When I studied psychology to get my doctorate from Biola University, I began to realize that too often the books I read, the leaders of various psychological theories I studied, did not take people deep enough. Because of that, their methods of therapy, though good, did not understand the core of humanity, the essential construct that makes a human a human - the soul.

This is what you will find so different in this book, my insight into the SOUL, your soul.

But more of this later.

In this book I will take you through three steps - three doors to healing that will cure you from worrying and anxiety.

The FIRST STEP or door will be based on cognitive therapy which, I believe, is the first great step to find healing. It is here that you work on thoughts and actions.

But I want to take you beyond this, beyond where most cognitive-behavioral therapist take you.

In the SECOND STEP and door, I will help you understand what beliefs are truly foundational to your life. Beliefs are thoughts that are rooted and thus impact any thoughts or actions you take.

This section of our 99¢ cure could very well open a new door for you and set you on a journey that will help to end your oppressive anxiety as you examine your beliefs.

But this still is not good enough. We want to cure your habitual anxiety once and for all, or at least give you the tools to handle it any time you begin to feel that overwhelming anxiety attack you and ruin your day.

In STEP THREE, or door 3, we will finally take you to a place where you can REALLY, FINALLY get healed. I will help you journey to the essential core of who you are and how this core can be renewed, refreshed and flow with continuous joy, happiness, hope and peace.

This is my goal in all of my 99¢ Cures books. And I deliver what you need…right now.

It will be incredible!

All for 99¢!

But you have to stay with me even when you feel a little resistant.

Make a commitment to take my three steps and go through the 3 doors I ask you to open and move through. I will have assignments I want you to do, things to repeat, thoughts to ponder. Work through these, and in a matter of days, maybe even today, the vice grip hold of your anxiety will begin to lesson, and soon, finally go away…

For Good!

PART ONE

Door Number 1
GETTING UNSTUCK

1

Breaking Loose

L OOK AT THE PICTURE.

You can see worry and anxiety on her face, can't you?

Let's call her Abby.

Abby has been stuck, sitting in that chair for days, weeks, maybe months. For most of the time the door was shut, and the room was dark.

But now Abby picks up my book, *Dr. Paul's 99¢ Cures.* She begins to read, and as she does, a faint glimmer of hope splashes across her face. She gets up, opens the door thinking:

Shall I go through that door, leave my safety in this dark space and venture out into another room or

Getting unstuck.

Breaking loose from the chains
that have held you in your anxiety.

This is what this section is about.

2

Misinterpretation of EVENTS, Past, Present And Future

———————

M OST PEOPLE SINCERELY BELIEVE THAT:

Events = Emotion

This belief keeps them stuck in their anxiety, in the darkness of inward worry and defeat. If you are anxious, you probably believe that this equation is true.

And it does make sense.

Someone you love leaves you (an event). This event seems to cause the anxiety you feel. You feel down and anxious about your life.

Or, you find you have cancer, lose a lot of money, a job, or someone says something hateful to you, and on and on. These are events that can cause emotional breakdown. There might be future events that you focus on and believe they may happen and cause disaster and as you do, the worry and anxiety levels rise.

Yet, and listen to me, you must get what I am to say, or you will be stuck in your anxiety.

Events (past, present or future) = **Emotion**
is a FALSE EQUATION

You see, no event or prediction of some future event can make you anxious.

Shocked? I hope so. I want to grab your attention and let you in on the secret too many do not know. Events do not cause your emotional feelings but rather your INTERPRETATION of the events whether past, present or future.

Stay with me so you can understand this.

In the first door, Abby was stuck in her prison of anxiety. Why? She blamed an event and was worried that event would keep repeating itself. But it wasn't the event that chained her to that chair and kept her in darkness. It was her INTERPRETATION of that event.

What event? It doesn't matter what event it may be. Events DO NOT have power over you. They are just happenings that cascade through our lives. The thing that does have power over you are your THOUGHTS about that event whether past, present or future.

Since this is true we can adjust our equation from:

$$\text{Events} = \text{Emotion}$$

To…

Events + INTERPRETATION

(of those events) **= Emotion**

Listen. It is YOUR INTERPRETATION of the event, past, present or future. that makes you anxious, swamped by anxiety and fear.

So then we can clearly state:

CHANGE YOUR INTERPRETATION
AND YOU WILL CHANGE YOUR EMOTION
(feelings of anxiety)

That's it!

"Ya, but," you say. "You don't know what happened or what might happen to me, the panic I feel, the money I lost, the person I loved who died or rejected me."

Give me any event and I can show you how to interpret it so you feel better.

Now I'm not saying that there should never be a time where you feel anxiety, where fear swamps you and you feel emotionally upended.

I know. I lost a wife to cancer after decades of marriage. I have had to battle 3 kinds of cancer that could have killed me. I had a financial advisor steal nearly $100,000 from my investments and battled through disappointments and anxiety of all kinds.

And there are times I get anxious.

Is this shocking since I am writing this book on how to cure it?

Let's get real. Worry and anxiety happens. Yet, we don't have to get trapped in a dark prison of anxiety for long. We can break out if we know what to do.

And what is it?

**CHANGE YOUR *INTERPRETATION*
AND YOU WILL CHANGE YOUR FEELINGS**

Your feelings are held hostage
by what you THINK and what you DO.

How do you change your interpretations?

Realize that INTERPRETATIONS are only THOUGHTS that come to you because of an event or fear of some future event. Something happens, your best friend turns against you, and you start thinking…thinking…thinking.

These thoughts are interpretations of the event, interpretations that will move you into anxiety or, if done right, will keep you from being totally devastated.

Let me take some events and show you how to change your thoughts from being destructive to thoughts that will bring hope and peace. We call this flipping (like flipping a switch from negative thoughts that will swamp you to thoughts that will encourage you).

This is also called reframing your thoughts so that the outcome will be one of hope instead of a gripping worry and anxiety.

The following are illustrations of how to do it. You can find a whole book I wrote that has thousands of illustrations on hundreds of subjects.

It's called: *Dr. Paul's FEELING GOOD ToolKit.*

You can find it at <u>DrPaulYoung.com</u>.

Read through the next few pages - illustrations of how you can change your INTERPRETATION and thus change your emotion.

EVENT	INTERPRETATONS FLIP IT REFRAIMING	EMOTION
Cancer	Why is this happening to me?	Anxiety
	How can I go on?	Anxiety
	I might die.	Fear
	God must hate me.	Disappointment
	I am going to learn from this experience.	Peace
	Thank God for the many people who are going to help me. I'm so lucky!	Peace. Gratitude
	If I die I'd go to heaven.	Hope
Lost my job	We are going to go broke and lose our home.	Anxiety
	This is unfair.	Anger

Event	Interpretations	Emotion
	I am going to work hard and find another job	Encouragement
	I am thankful for the job I did have.	Gratitude
Investment down	I won't be able to retire.	Anxiety
	Who is going to take care of me?	Confusion
	I give up.	Anxiety
	Stocks will come back. They always do.	Hope.
	Delayed retirement doesn't mean I can't enjoy my life.	Encouragement

EVENT	**INTERPRETATIONS FLIP IT, REFRAMING**	**EMOTION**
Problem Children	Why did I ever have kids?	Anger
	I feel so rejected.	Anxiety
	They don't treat me right.	Resentment
	No matter what they do, I will show my love to them.	Determination

	Even though they are not behaving the right way, I choose to love them and thank God for them.	Joy Peace
Health Problems	I'm sick of being sick!	Anxiety
	Why me?	Anxiety
	I feel miserable all the time.	Resentment
	Why does God let bad things happen to good people? This sucks!	Doubt
	At least I'm alive!	Hope
	I will not let my sickness define who I am.	Determination
	I will focus on the many other good things I have and not my sickness.	Peace Gratitude
	What can I learn from my sickness?	Anticipation
People Problems	Why do they act like jerks?	Anger
	I will never talk with them again.	Resentment Bitterness
	I have no true friends.	Anxiety

	I will continue to be a friend.	Determination
	Though others may reject me, I accept myself and know that I am a good person.	Hope
	I will find a good friend if I keep being a loving, friendly person.	Happiness
Father is a jerk.	Why did I get such a jerk of a father?	Anxiety
	When will he ever learn to treat me right?	Misery
	My dad's a jerk, but I still love him.	Hope
	I will always show outward love to my father through my actions and words.	Determination
	Though my dad acts like a jerk at times, I choose to thank God for my dad.	Joy Gratitude
Work Problems	I hate this job!	Anger Frustration Disgust
	I'll never get ahead.	Anxiety

EVENT	INTERPRETATIONS FLIP IT, REFRAMING	EMOTION
	It's 12 years before I can retire.	Anxiety
	The pay is miserable.	Discouragement
	At least I have a job!	Gratefulness
	If I am patient, I can find a better job.	Hope
	Though I have a sad job, I choose to be happy.	Joy
	The pain I feel is going to make me a better person.	Peace
EVENT	**INTERPRETATIONS FLIP IT, REFRAMING**	**EMOTION**
My husband died	I can't make it.	Anxiety
	I wish I were dead.	Anxiety
	I hurt so much.	Grief
	"God. Why did you let this happen?"	Anger
	Thank you God for letting us live this long together.	Gratitude
	I will miss him terribly, but I will make it and find joy again.	Hope

EVENT	INTERPRETATIONS FLIP IT, REFRAMING	EMOTION
	He's in heaven and having a great time.	Joy Peace
I have no real friends	I'm worthless.	Anxiety
	No one likes me.	Worthlessness
	Nothing will ever change.	Anxiety
	Until I find a friend, I will be a friend to myself.	Peace
	I will go to church and join a group.	Hope
	I will stop moping and start coping!	Determination
	I will make someone a great friend!	Confidence Joy
EVENT	**INTERPRETATIONS FLIP IT, REFRAMING**	**EMOTION**
Look how much I weigh!	I'm a failure.	Failure
	To be liked, I must be thin.	Anxiety
	Fat is ugly.	Anxiety
	Fat is beautiful!	Joy
	I choose to be happy though fat!	Glad

	My joy is not dependent on how much I weigh.	Peace
Constant problems	Why is life so hard?	Disappointment
	Nothing seems to turn out right.	Anxiety
	I just feel such a weight.	Despair
	God is unfair.	Anger
	These weighty problems are really exciting challenges.	Hope
	Anything is possible if I don't quit.	Encouragement
	Complaining only brings misery. I will stop complaining for a day.	Peace
	I will quit fixing the blame and fix the problem.	Confidence

Now write out the events that you are going through right now. Take each event and come up with some interpretations that will bring hope.

As you do this, always tell yourself the truth. You are not trying to distort what is happening to you, only seeking to come up with another way of looking at it, a way that will bring courage, hope, peace and even joy.

Remember, it is not the event that has brought the anxiety but the way you interpreted that event.

Practice now:

Name the EVENT or coming things that are causing you anxiety. Come up with some INTERPRETATIONS - ways of viewing that present or future event or happening in a way that will produce emotions that lift you up rather than defeat you.

Remember:

CHANGE YOUR *INTERPRETATION*
AND YOU WILL CHANGE HOW YOU FEEL

Event	**Interpretation**	**Emotion**
1.		
2.		
3.		
4.		
5.		
6.		
7.		

3

Become An Actor or Actress

N COGNITIVE-BEHAVIORAL THERAPY, it is not just **THOUGHTS** that change how you feel but **ACTIONS**. When you take action steps, something is triggered in the brain. Your thoughts begin to change relative to the action steps you take.

It's magical!

For example, when you are anxious, put a big smile on your face, or laugh. These action steps actually trigger a response in your brain that sends new messages to your emotions and you actually feel better.

It's not that you want to do something that is not in line with the truth. Yes, you are anxious. But your desired end is to stop that anxiety. How?

Change your thoughts and your actions. When you act in a way in line with how you WANT to feel (though you are not feeling that way now) you will, with certainty, change how you feel.

Many anxious people slump when they sit or stand.

ACTION: Stand or sit up straight.   Put your shoulders back like you are confident.

Other anxious people breathe shallow breaths.

ACTION: Take deep breaths.   Hold the breath for a few seconds, then let it out slowly.   Do this for three minutes.

Many anxious people never smile or laugh.

ACTION: Put a big smile on your face and laugh for one minute.   Laughing actually massages your internal organs and releases a natural drug that makes you happy.   So laugh!

You may say that you don't feel like it.

Of course you don't. That is why these action steps are so important.   They force you to do something that you do not want to do, but in doing it, bring about change - a release, even for a moment, from your anxiety.

Remember: When you connect this action with a change of your interpretation, it's powerful!

Look at some examples below:

EVENT	ACTION	EMOTION
LOST JOB	Smile	Hopeful
	Look for job	Determination
	Focus on heart's desires for job	Excitement
	Laugh/Dance	Joy
	Relax/Deep breaths	Peace
	Go for a walk	Calm
HUSBAND IS A JERK	Write out his 20 positive attributes and share them with him	Caring
	Write out a list of 10 ways you can please him and do them one at a time	Determination
	Smile/Laugh/Dance	Joy
	Focus on fun with girlfriends	Anticipation
	Counter his jerkiness with love	Brave
	Give a blessing for a curse	Love
NEWS IS BAD	Turn off the news	Less anxiety
	Play uplifting music	Joy
	Focus on the good news	Hopeful
	Google good news	Inspired

	Turn on the radio and listen to music	Calming
	Laugh for one minute. Do this 10 times today	Pleasure
CANCER	Smile. Say: "I've got cancer but cancer doesn't have me!"	Determination
	Cry (It is never good to repress actions that flow from a terrible event. Grief, anger, anxiety, anxiety, loneliness and other emotional responses are healthy. They become UNHEALTHY, though when we hang on to them for an extended period of time. You must be honest and truthful in your approach to writing out interpretations and actions)	Release anxiety
	Shout: "I'm going to win! Cancer is going to lose!"	Hope
	Laugh	Daring
	Write a list of things and people you are grateful for	Thanksgiving
	Become part of a support group	Encouragement
INVESTMENT DOWN	Practice deep breathing	Peace

	Smile	Joy
	Laugh	Optimistic
	Shout: "I'm down but not out!"	Hopeful
	Go for a walk	Calming
PROBLEMS WITH FAMILY, WORK, FRIENDS, MOTHER, HEALTH	Stop complaining!	Relaxed
	Get off your butt and do something!	Determination
	Write out a list of your problems and what you plan on DOING about it	Hopeful
	Quite bitching and start blessing	Joyful
	Focus on blessing	Gratefulness
	Write out a list of all the good things about your family, work, friends, mother, health, etc.	Positive
	Smile, laugh, breathe, shout, dance	Liberated
	Walk, eat good foods for your brain (omega 3), build strong social networks, walk, workout, listen to music	All these things bring a calm to the brain and peace to the soul
HUSBAND DIED	Cry	Release tension
	Smile	Gratefulness

	Say: " Thank God he isn't suffering anymore."	Thankful
	List all the good attributes he had	Grateful
	Say: "I will make it."	Determination
	Buy a bird, dog, cat, fish	Fills up that lonely space
	Be with family/friends	Calm
TIRED	Breathe	Peace
	Smile	Joy
	Take a nap	Hope
	Go for a slow walk	Energizes
	Eat foods that give energy	Determination

These are just some sample ways to use ACTION steps to break you out of the prison of worry and anxiety.

Now, write out some action steps that will help you break free from your anxiety.

EVENT.	ACTION	EMOTION
1.		
2.		
3.		

4.

5.

This is not easy to do. But if you are going to be joyful again, work at it, and success will be yours! You will finally not only be cured, but know how to cure yourself when anxiety comes knocking at your door again.

THOUGHTS + ACTIONS = EMOTION

Change your thoughts and actions and you will FEEL better again.[1]

---

[1] If you want to go deeper into this topic, you can read through my **Dr. Paul's TOTAL Relief - Depression**. It is a series of books, workbooks and YES! Cards that will help you immensely. Though the subject is depression, these books have helped many work through their anxiety and fears. It's worth a try!

Also, my book, **Dr. Paul's FEELING GOOD ToolKit** lists hundreds of areas that open the door to anxiety and how to THINK and ACT in each situation. It will be a big help to you.

And all these books, if bought together (10 books total), will cost you a fraction of the fees you would pay if you had a personal session with me or any psychotherapist.

PART 2

Door Number 2
EMBRACING LOVE

1

Core Beliefs

IN DOOR NUMBER 1, WE SAW ABBY MOVING from the chair of anxiety that held her in a prison of darkness and panic and defeat. That ended when she opened the door and let some light on her situation. From there she learned how to have proper THOUGHTS and ACTIONS. Learning this began to bring an end to her worry and anxiety.

But there was a reoccurring difficulty, her core beliefs.

Beliefs are simply thoughts that are rooted, and when one of your core beliefs is at odds with what is true, it will sabotage your thoughts and thus your emotions.

For example, if Abby felt that she was not worthy of being loved, then that belief would sabotage all her work in developing thoughts that would get her out of her anxiety.

Some core beliefs are:

BELIEFS	FEELINGS
I am good	Competent
I am bad	Miserable
As a person, I am significant	Loved
I'm nobody	Worthless
I can weather any difficulty	Confidence
I am loved (by God and others)	Secure
I belong	Acceptance
No one loves me for who I am	Anxiety
I am competent	Confidence
I'm a failure	Shame
I'm ugly	Useless
I'm fun to be with	Joy
I can make it through any circumstance	Hopeful
Nothing ever turns out right	Despair
Life is difficult, but I have help from God and others	Determination

Dig deep and come up with some of your core beliefs and write what kind of feelings those beliefs are producing

BELIEFS   **FEELINGS**

1.

2.

3.
4.

5.

6.

7.

9.

10.

2

THE GREATEST CORE BELIEF

THERE ARE MANY GOOD AND WORTHWHILE CORE BELIEFS that can help you break out of anxiety and find relief.

If you believe that you are a person worth loving, and feel that love, it means that there are thoughts that are rooted deep in your heart.   These thoughts that you have interpret reality, telling you that you are a person of worth, a person of significance, and a person who has value.

"SOMEONE LOVES ME!" your heart screams out.

You know it. It is a settled fact. There is proof. My father, mother, husband, wife, friends, relatives and work associates love me.

It may not be all of them. It never is. But SOMEONE loves me. There is ample evidence, enough to make this a settled truth, a BELIEF.

You see, the **ONE CORE BELIEF** THAT CHANGES EVERYTHING IS:

LOVE!

THIS FOUNDATION BELIEF IS THE MOST VITAL CORE BELIEF. The person who is loved will always find a way to smile, to break through the clouds of trouble, conflict and disaster, and find peace and joy.

Isn't this what you want with all your heart?

Of course!

And believe me, I know how to get you there, not because I'm so smart, but because I know the path, the narrow path to take you there, the path that will bring you to the CURE FOR YOUR Anxiety.

As I have said before, there are many other paths that can bring some relief. You can change your THOUGHTS and ACTIONS and learn how to INTERPRET any event whether past, present or future, so you can change your feelings.

But that will only take you so far. Stepping through door 1, and finally getting unstuck, breaking out of the prison of misinterpretations that have kept you behind the bars of darkness and anxiety is great. How can it be better?

But it can.

Too often people only go this far and never experience the totality of joy, hope and peace they were made to enjoy. Why? They do not have a good foundational belief that someone loves them deeply and feels that they are valuable, significant and important.

This is why this core belief of LOVE is so important.

Let me help you understand it so that you can move through this door and fully embrace this belief, a belief that can be yours…guaranteed!

Abby went through the door of love and found something surprising. You can find it too!

Our hearts ache to be fully loved - totally, completely.

There are three different types of love.

1. **I love you "if" kind of love.** "If you will do this for me, I will love you."

This is purely conditional love. It puts you under the microscope and examines everything you are and do.

2. **I love you "because of" kind of love.** This is another conditional kind of love, but better than the "if" kind. It goes this way: "I love you because you are beautiful."

But what happens if in an accident that beauty is marred?   Love then evaporates.   Or..."I love you because of your sense of humor." Yet, what happens if this person suffers some kind of mental injury either by accident or disease? Are they still loved?

There is nothing wrong with loving a person because of beauty, humor, or any other positive trait. But this can't be a foundational and an enduring kind of love.

3. **I love you "no matter what" kind of love.** Now this kind of love will last. We want to be loved this way, that no matter what happens, that person who declared their love for us will keep on loving us..."no matter what."

This is the kind of love that sacrifices for the person loved.

You remember that Abby's husband left her for another woman. Why? His love was an "if" kind of love as he found another woman who gave HIM what he wanted. This kind of love is selfish and self-centered. When Abby's husband left her, he, in fact, showed that he never ever really loved Abby.

Though the marriage ended in divorce - not what Abby wanted, but she didn't have to live with a selfish, self-centered person the rest of her life, a very good thing.

Once she realized this, she was able to take this terrible event, her husband leaving for another woman and see the good that came from it. She was saved from years of anxiety and misery.

Yet could Abby ever find someone who would truly love her?

The problem lies in this: Most humans are weak and imperfect. Thus their love is imperfect.

Where, then, could Abby find a love that is worth trusting, giving her life to it without fear of being let down?

Read on.

3

GOD LOVES YOU!

Abby WAS MARRIED TO THE LOVE OF HER LIFE. Then, after a few years of marriage, this one she loved so much ran off with another woman, devastating her. "How could he do this," she sobbed? And through it all she began to wonder if anyone would ever love her again.

"Can anyone truly love me?"

All of this causes loads of anxiety and can keep us awake at night, make us want to eat foods that, after weight gain, cause even further anxiety. Or we lie awake at night and suffer from sleep deprivation.

So the question, "Can anyone truly love me" is a question we all ask at times? If we do not feel someone loves us, our hearts will ache most of our lives, chained to thoughts of inadequacy, anxiety and fear.

So many die of a broken heart because they do not feel loved.   Others are covered over with such fear and anxiety that it creates a load of health issues that can greatly impact their lives.

Is that you?   Is your heart broken or are you full of fear most of the time?   Do you know that someone truly loves you?   And…are you worth being loved, protected and taken care of?

You see the bold statement at the head of this chapter - God loves **YOU!** But is that true? Is that only kind of like a Santa Claus myth that is just a feel good story that is not in line with reality?

Does God really love you?

Don't shove this question aside thinking that you are not interested in religion at all.   To sweep God from your thoughts ultimately gets rid of all meaning and purpose in life. Why are you here? Who made you? Are you only a composite of organisms that came from an impersonal universe?

If you believe this, look at my book, *If There Is A God, Whose God is God?* It will help you think through you and God in a very logical way. I think you will like it.

This will open your heart to a love that can change your life.

The Holy Scriptures say: *GOD IS LOVE.*

This is essentially who he is…PURE LOVE.

And it's not the kind of love that is an "if" or a "because of" kind of love. Yes, it is true that God gives us laws and principles to live by, but only because he loves us. He never says: "You screw up and I will hate you."

Never!

The Scriptures state this:

> *God **PROVED HIS LOVE** FOR US that while we were sinners (doing things that are wrong - things that hurt us and others), Christ DIED for us.*
>
> Romans 5

Now that's the kind of love to build your life on, the kind to believe in.

God's love is ALWAYS giving.

> *God so loved the world that he **GAVE** his only begotten Son.*
>
> John 3

St. Peter wrote:

*Cast all you care on God for **HE CARES** for you.*
                    I Peter 5

"Yet," people say, "if God loved me, why did this horrible thing happen?" Or, "If God loves me now, why am I facing all this trouble in the future? Why doesn't God give me everything I want?"

It's like Abby saying: "If God loved me, why did he let my husband leave me for another woman?"

You already know the answer, don't you?

You see what kind of jerk her husband was, and if that marriage continued, Abby would have been constantly hurt. So GOD, IN LOVE, SAVED HER from what would have been a long term, miserable marriage.

There is the age old question that states: "If God loves me and also has all power to stop anything, why did he let this horrible thing (like cancer, death of a child, loss of job, accident that left permanent scars, rape, divorce, etc.) happen to me?

First, God is love.

Second, God is all powerful.

Realize that God often does not stop our suffering and pain because HE DIDN'T STOP HIS SUFFERING and pain. Why? Suffering on his part and ours can be redemptive and bring about eternal and glorious changes both to us and others.

This is why in the Catholic and some other churches Jesus Christ is still on the cross in full display to all who enter. Why? How grotesque!

Really?

Jesus said:

> *Greater love has no one for another than a person who gives his life for his friend.*
>
> John 15

This is how much God loves you and me. God GAVE HIS ALL that we might find life to the full.

In the book of 1st Corinthians, chapter 10, St. Paul writes these words:

> *There is no test or problem that you face that is not uncommon to others too. We all have had problems in the past and will face difficulty in the future. BUT GOD IS FAITHFUL (because he loves you) and will not let any present or future difficulty bring you to the breaking point. He will ALWAYS, IN LOVE, PROVIDE*

A WAY OUT *so that you might be able to bear up under the load and come out successful.*

I Cor. 10: 13 personalized

It is so important to understand God's love, that he is NEVER OUT TO HURT US but to HELP us...guaranteed!

If you do not grasp God's love and bank your life on it, you may ALWAYS struggle with some form of fear and anxiety. Instead, when you have a core belief that God WILL NOT LET ANYTHING TOUCH YOU UNLESS IT IS FOR YOUR BEST, you then will be free from worry and anxiety.

Yes, you can practice reinterpreting every event so that your feelings will change. Great! But that is not enough. If you want to move into a deeper kind of joy and inner happiness, you need to embrace the LOVE OF GOD.

I have sent people to a Catholic Church and spend time before the crucifix. I ask them to spend at least 15 minutes drinking in the love of God.

Go ahead, touch his wounds like Thomas did. It was in the touching of the wounds of Christ that he found new life, hope and even a new mission that drove him to India to share the good news about the love of God.

When a person goes into a Catholic Church they will see a red light (a candle) burning. This means that Jesus is present in the Tabernacle - a special place where they put the Eucharist - the actual body of Jesus Christ.

If you do this, you can ask this Jesus who is present to show you more fully his love for YOU.

He doesn't just love the world…he loves YOU! Drink it in. And let this be a belief that will be a foundation that will not be shaken.

Say: "GOD LOVES ME!"

Shout it out!

Knowing this will dispel your anxiety - all the nasty things that have occurred to you, or you feel might occur to you. All the bitter hassles were allowed to touch you so that you might lean more fully on the love of God.

Abby when to a Catholic Church and was changed in the process. It was there she had a conversion of heart as she realized for the first time the love of God. All the hurt ultimately came to bring her into the arms of a loving God who loved her deeply and wanted her to trust him completely.

All her anxiety about the future based on the past action of others began to dissipate.

Why does God allow hurt and pain? It is ultimately to heal us, to take us to another level in our lives, to reach the mountain top struggling all the way, yet when we make it to the top there is unequalled joy.

Wow!

What love!

Now, think about your life and answer these questions:

1. Have you ever really been truly loved?
2. Who, without question, loves you today, without strings attached, no conditions?
3. Do you really believe that God loves you? If so, why? If not, why not?
4. What is keeping you from embracing his love?
5. Are you willing to go to a Catholic Church and spend time, in front of the crucifix, meditating on Christ's love for you?
6. How can this core belief of God's love dispel your anxiety?

Part 3

Door Number 3
OPENING YOUR SOUL

1

Opening The Door To God

Abby HAS GONE THROUGH TWO DOORS. The first door she went through broke her from the darkness and chains of anxiety and brought her into a room filled with light and understanding. It was here that she began to reinterpret every event that happened to her, events in the present and future that she feared.

It was life-changing!

Then she moved through the second door of love - choosing to accept and embrace the LOVE of God and to know that this God would let NOTHING TOUCH HER unless it was for her good.

Period!

The changes she made in her life equalled a miracle.

Change is not always easy. For many, it is easy to sit in their chair of anxiety (again see door 1) rather than move into another sphere that is not familiar to them. Their anxiety is familiar. They are at home with it, since they have lived with it a long time.

Yet Abby did not stay stuck in the darkness. Venturing out into the light took courage, and so too for you.

Hopefully you have come this far and taken giant leaps toward beating back your anxiety. Now, though, there is one final step, another door to go through that could change everything…for good.

Abby walked through that open door to God. She knew he loved her. But she wanted more. She wanted to know him better on a friendship level deep within her soul.

Soul, you ask?

Why do we need God in our souls?

2

True Psychology

WE ALL THINK WE KNOW WHAT PSYCHOLOGY IS. REALLY? Most do not know that the word comes from the Greek word "psyche," a word for the SOUL. Yet when you go to a psychologist or therapist, you will find that many have never studied the soul.

Because of this, most psychotherapists only take people part of the way to TOTAL recovery thus leaving their client only partially healed. They do not understand the true makeup of a person, that internal part that is left empty and alienated.

It is a shame that most universities where psychologists are trained never address this internal part of humanity. Why? It's simple. They refuse to study the soul, that very thing that psychology (SOULcology - the study of the soul) should be studying. But it is off limits at most universities. They avoid this study due to an antagonism against religion and any mention that brings God into the picture.

What happens? In avoiding the study of the soul, they take those suffering from anxiety only part of the way to healing and don't bring TOTAL Relief.

I wrote a series of books including workbooks and helpful "YES!" Cards to counter what too many therapists offer their clients - some even Christian, who are swept up in a more secular approach rather than leading each client on a pathway that will open their souls to God and his unmatched presence and love.[2]

It was the great St. Augustine who said:

Thou hast made us for thyself and our hearts are restless until they find their rest in thee.

Jesus said:

Come to me all who weary and laden with heavy burdens, and I will give you rest for your souls.
Matt. 11

Soul rest. Now that's where real healing takes place.

---

[2] These books, **Dr. Paul's TOTAL RELIEF - Depression**, are very applicable to those who suffer from worry and anxiety. The "Yes!" Cards are really great for dispelling that crippling anxiety. Look these up. They might be the thing that helps you. There are also great helps on my website that address these issues, CURE CARDS and STEP BY STEP plans to cure what ails you. See DrPaulPress.com

Abby had gone through door number one and learned how to think and act - reinterpreting each event so that she didn't feel bad and taking actions steps that reinforced those new thoughts.

Then she embraced the love of God accepting that any event that came her way, God allowed, in his love, to help her, not hurt her.

Now she needed to go through this final door and open her soul to God.

Abby had come so far since being swamped by her anxiety when her husband left her for another woman. Everything had turned dark spurred on by his rejection. She felt worthless and unworthy...until she saw how much God loved her and spoke clearly to her about her value, a value more than all the assets of the world, that value of her soul.

Abby had discovered TRUE PSYCHOLOGY and her SOUL was being changed.[3]

---

[3]Book 3 of Dr. Paul's TOTAL Relief - Depression, goes a lot more in depth than this short work. You will learn the difference between an animal soul and a human soul and how that impacts you.

3

The Breath of God

O YOU REALIZE THAT THE WORD "SOUL" CAN ALSO BE TRANSLATED "BREATH?" Amazing, isn't it that the one essential thing we have to live is not food or water, but BREATH. This is the vital force that animates our bodies and is the seat of our emotions (feelings), will (action) and thoughts.

It is here that a person is distinguished from any other person, their uniqueness as designed by God.

It's interesting that we find in the creation account in Genesis that God BREATHED into Adam and Eve, and they became living SOULS.

No wonder so many relaxation techniques focus on the breath. Yet, even in this, they emphasize human breath rather than the breath of God breathing into our souls, bringing life, hope, joy and peace.

In my counseling, I have found that many who come to me have never fully spent time breathing in the presence and love of God. No wonder there is so much emptiness and anxiety!

Years ago, while on a water skiing trip with some Christian teens, one of them challenged me to see if I could hold my breath as long as he.   I accepted the challenge. He went under water and held his breath for a minute and a half. I did the same and bested his mark to a minute and 40 seconds.

He then held his breath for 2 minutes. I went under the water and held my breath for 2 1/2 minutes.   He countered by 2 3/4 minutes.

Finally, I went under the water holding my breath. As I got to the 2 1/2 I felt my chest heaving, gasping for air. Then I heard them say 2 3/4 and then finally 3 minutes. I came out of the water desperately in need of air - to breathe again lest I die!

Breath. How vital it is. How necessary to living.

Yet, this essential, the breath of God, is neglected. We breathe oxygen but never this heavenly breath from a God who wants to breathe into us every day, every hour, every moment, his life.

You see, I was able to hold my breath for 3 minutes and was ready to die!

How long do we hold the breath of our souls without being nourished by God himself - a day, a week, a month, even years?   No wonder there is so much depression, anxiety and fear.   Very few are filling their souls with the breath of God.

How do we do this? Keep reading.

4

Filling The Soul With God

Abby WAS MAKING GOOD PROGRESS TOWARD GETTING OVER HER ANXIETY. Yet she had this final door to go through. She went to church and prayed some, but when I talked with her about the soul, she knew that she had a long way to go.

You need to take care of your soul, and you will take care of your anxiety. Why? Disturbance here will ripple through your whole person - your thoughts, actions and beliefs. Drink in the daily breath of God and, even through the hurts and disasters of life, you will be at peace with a joy that is unspeakable.

St. Peter said:

> Though you have not seen *him, you love him; and even though you do not see I'm now, you believe in him and are filled with an inexpressible and glorious joy...*
>
> I Peter 1:8-9

Did you get that…INEXPRESSIBLE AND GLORIOUS JOY!

This is what all anxious people desire…JOY, an inner happiness and peace that will not go away.

The secret: Being filled in your soul. When your soul if filled, this joy and peace becomes automatic. And it comes…

>   Not by just doing something
>   But by being *with* SOMEONE

Christianity is not just a set of rules, beliefs and behaviors, but is essentially a RELATIONSHIP with God the Father, his Son, Jesus Christ and the Holy Spirit - all three want to fill your soul!

Awesome!

You see, **Door 1**, we learn how to think and act the right way, a way that changes how we feel.

In **Door 2**, we looked at our core beliefs and saw that the belief that will change our life the most is embracing the LOVE of God. He is never out to hurt us but help us (though that sometimes hurts). He is always out to make us better, His love insures that.

So no matter what happened in the past, what will happen today or in the future, God has you covered.

Relax.   Take a deep breath.   And then move on to breathing in the life, love, and peace of God which passes all understanding[4]

In **Door 3**, we are brought to see our most essential self - our soul and learning how to breathe in the breath of God.   His breath gives life abundant, life to the full resulting in inexpressible, indescribable, unspeakable, unfathomable glorious, magnificent, dazzling, awesome, remarkable, sensational, gratifying JOY!

It is here that his thoughts become our thoughts and his ways become our ways. There becomes a blending of our natures as we share in his divine life.

Some circles of Christianity call this the EXCHANGED LIFE - he in us and we in him.

Abby asked: "How does this happen? What can I do to fill my soul so that I don't feel this emptiness anymore?

"One of the answers is found in the Gospel of John," I said.

I then went on and related this information.

In the Gospel of John Jesus asked a couple of men,

---

[4] I have a great book for you to read that will supplement what you are reading here. It's called **4 STEPS TO PEACE**. It is a book that is based on Philippians 4:6-7. Read it. It could change your life!

"What do you want?"

This is one of the greatest questions that was ever asked.

King Solomon was told by God that he would give him "whatever he wanted." And, to paraphrase his answer, he asked that he might have a deep relationship with God, that he could hear him with the ears of his heart.

When Jesus asked these two men this question, they gave the GREATEST answer one could give, an answer in line with King Solomon's wish. These men said:

> *We want to know where you live - where you abide.*
>
> John 1

Now on the surface this doesn't seem very deep. But these men were not asking for Jesus' address, but instead they were looking for the opportunity to spend time with him - at his place, his residence, his home.

They wanted to be AT HOME WITH JESUS.

So Jesus took them, these 2 men, only 2 men, to his home. And they started a revolution that changed the world.

Within a day these 2 men reached another 2 men, and on and on. By the time Jesus died there were over 500, then

3,000, then 8,000 and soon there were over 50,000 in Jerusalem who had become followers of Jesus.

How did it happen?

Two guys who wanted to spend time with Jesus.

That's all. They wanted to be JOHN 15 men (read this chapter - it's amazing). They wanted to abide with Christ.

You see, you can't spend time with Jesus and nothing else happens.   In that quiet time with him you are transformed, made into one of his revolutionaries, a disciple who becomes an IMPACT person.

But, IT ALL STARTS WITH TIME WITH JESUS.

You start with Jesus - listening to him in the Gospels, or in the Psalms, or the book of Philippians, or any other book of the Bible, journaling, praying, opening your heart to his desires, confessing your sin, sharing with him you deepest concerns.

It is in this time that you become friends that meet each day. And it is from this time together that something happens to you. You are changed deep within your soul and want to impact others.

So...WHAT DO YOU WANT?

Abby said: "I want more of Jesus."

"Then," I responded, "spend time with him is Scripture (read the Gospels), in prayer, and, if Catholic, before the Blessed Sacrament, seeing Jesus in the bread and wine and receiving the TOTAL Christ, both spiritually and physically (in bread and wine which is transformed into his body and blood).

Too many Christians only receive Jesus spiritually. And this is great! Keep doing that. But also consider what the early Christians did, received him also physically in the bread and wine.

Jesus did not come just spiritually. The incarnation means he took upon himself true flesh. The real Jesus is not just a spirit, but a body and spirit. Receive both of them in the Eucharist in the Catholic Church. It can make all the difference. The TOTAL JESUS comes to rest in your soul.

Next I gave Abby this outline of how to read Scripture in a special way, a way that opens the SOUL to Jesus. Reading this way will slowly rid your soul of all the anxiety you feel.

Lectio Divina

ectio Divina is a slow, prayerful, meditative, contemplative approach to the Scriptures. Lectio Divina means "divine reading." It is a very old practice in the Church and goes back to St. Benedict in the 6th century. There are rules you must follow to practice Lectio Divina. It is an approach to Holy Scripture that is:

1. **SLOW.** You are not out to read an entire section, chapter or even a paragraph. You go word by word, drinking in the meaning, pausing as you observe this word of God to you. You don't want to miss anything. You have prayed: "Open my eyes that I may see wondrous things out of your word" (Psalm 119), and you believe that this will come to pass. You are centering on HIM, your creator, your master, your intimate friend.

It may take you a week, two weeks, a month to get through a chapter. But that's OK. It's not how much of the bible you get through that counts but how much of the bible gets into you. This is a treasure hunt where you are looking under every word for that special treasure God has for you. It is like squeezing an orange, desiring to get out all the juice, the sweetness into your soul. You are seeking to merge your thoughts with HIS thoughts. So you quiet your mind, find a place where you can leisurely loiter in the presence of the God who wants to embrace you, guide you, and be your friend.

2. **PRAYERFUL.** It is here in the Scriptures that we meet face to face with God. He wants to enfold us into a deep relationship with him. So we pray, "Come Father, come Holy Spirit, come Lord Jesus and meet me as I drink in your precious words." It is in this process that we find that Jesus will "open our minds to understand the Scriptures," like he did those early two disciples on the road to Emmaus. So as we read the Holy Scriptures, we are always praying, communicating with the God who gave us his word.

The Scriptures are like a telescope that bring us into the presence of God. Too often people study the telescope, take it apart, know all about how it functions and works. And that may be good, but the ultimate purpose of a telescope is to bring a person into the presence of the stars. So too the Scriptures. You can study them, memorize them, read them, tear them apart, but until you let them bring you into the presence of Jesus, you are not using them the way they were designed.

This is why, when we open this sacred book, we pray and keep on praying. The words of Scripture are not ordinary words. They are powerful, explosive, life changing. And we cannot come with human understanding and think we will grasp what these words mean. We must tune our ears to the writer of these words, God himself, talking with him, and letting him talk with us.

3. **MEDITATIVE.** Here we are ruminating, marinating, chewing, rolling over the words of Scripture in our minds and hearts. During this time we are talking with God and letting him talk with us. The "ears on our hearts" like Solomon, are attentive, ready to receive insight, the kind that produces a "burning in our hearts," like it did on those two early disciples with Jesus. At this point we begin direct dialogue with God, interacting, drinking, eating, breathing in his words, letting our souls consume them, this spiritual nourishment that is vital to our spiritual existence. God is becoming our friend in an intimacy that cannot be described, so deep it is, so close, so loving. We share with him our deepest desires, our hopes, our dreams, our pain, our doubts, our confidence in him. And we listen, drinking in his words in the moment, *rhema,* hot bread for the soul that results in joy and inner gladness.

King David in Psalm 1, talks about ruminating on the Scriptures day and night. I recommend people memorize sections of Scriptures as they work through them, words of God that they can sift through in their minds and hearts through the day. Like a cow chewing its cud, we can chew on the Word of God, slowly, meditatively, getting out of it all the nourishment that is needed for that moment.

4. **CONTEMPLATIVE.** You are swept into a place of total reverence, praise and joy. You drink it in, not saying anything, not listening at this point, just lingering, resting in HIS presence. There is a total silence, yet a communication that goes beyond words taking us into infinity, into the realm of God, into his throne room, the holy of holies. It is like two lovers who embrace without saying any words. The moment has swept them into an encounter of their souls. So too with God. He is in us, we in him, in that infinite, finite embrace.

It is like mouth to mouth resuscitation. We receive his life. At this point we may hear the groans of the Holy Spirit that St. Paul talks about in Romans 8, uttering words that we cannot understand. It is awesome, breathtaking, magnificent, overwhelming and absolutely necessary if we are going to get back to the Garden of Eden where we lost this great gift, communing with and embracing our creator.

This brings about the change we need, a change that breathes into us HIS life.

Making sure that Abby had sufficient tools so that she could open her soul to the breath of God, I also gave her this helpful approach to opening any Scriptural text.

THE FIVE QUESTIONS Method
TO READING THE SCRIPTURE
(Can be used with the daily readings)

When you read a specific Scripture or focus on the daily readings like The WORD Among Us, MAGNIFICAT, or others, ask the following five questions. They will help you to dig deeper and allow you to benefit greatly with your time with God. It is best to read a paragraph or two as you do this.

1. What is a **KEY WORD,** words or phrase that stands out when I read this passage? Look it up in the dictionary to get its clear meaning or use biblehub.com.

2. In a **SENTENCE** or two, what is the passage talking about?

3. Can I **ILLUSTRATE** what the passage is talking about in my own life or in the life of another?

4. What is Jesus **ASKING ME TO DO** in response to this passage?

5. If Jesus were standing before me right now (and he is!) and asked me: "**WHAT DO YOU WANT** me to do for you?" What would I say?

Write these answers down in your journal.   It's life changing!

Jesus stands at the door of your life, your soul and wants to come in. Listen to him as he says:

> Look. I stand at the door of your soul and would like to come in. I won't force myself in. You must invite me into your life. If you do, I will come in and feed you in a way that you have never been fed before. You will delight in my presence and your soul will finally be at peace, and experience hope and joy.

5

The Miracle of Praise

WHEN YOU DISCOVER TRUE PSYCHOLOGY AND THE VALUE OF YOUR SOUL, you will never be the same. You will begin to develop a relationship with your creator, the one who started the human race by BREATHING INTO THEM, and they became living souls.

Once you understand the magic of this, this depth that is missed in most therapy sessions in the world, you will begin to come to a place where true healing will occur. Your soul will be finally liberated to become all the creator intended - and that will free it to find, as the Psalmist said:

PLEASURES FOR EVER!
Psalm 16

When you begin to feel this joy, your heart will begin to sing praises to God. He, your eternal lover, has satisfied your soul and you lift up your hands, clap, shout, blast the trumpet as you praise him.

Look at all the praise Psalms in Scripture. They come from hearts that are full and overflowing with gratitude to God.

There is something magical that happens to you when you begin to praise God. A power is released in your mind and emotions that cannot be matched by any other exercise.

People take drugs to imitate this kind of feeling. And they may get it for a moment or two. Then, back to the drugs for another hit - hoping, grasping, longing for a joy and peace that will never end.

But in God is FULLNESS of peace and joy. Living in HIS PRESENCE, breathing in his nature is all that is needed to release the human spirit to fly high, to move beyond the grips of anxiety and despair.

Praise chases away your worry and anxiety.

Praise.

There is such power in it.

Praise the LORD (Psalm 150)

Hallelujah!
Praise God **in** His sanctuary
Praise Him **in** the firmament of his power
Praise God **for** His mighty acts
Praise Him **according to** His abundant greatness
Praise Him **with** the blast of the horn
Praise Him **with** the psaltery and harp
Praise Him **with** the timbrel and dance
Praise Him **with** stringed instruments and the pipe
Praise him **with** the loud-sounding cymbals
Praise Him **with** the clanging cymbals
Let every thing that hath breath
PRAISE THE LORD!
Hallelujah!

You may also want to praise God in music. Sing to him.
Put on some CD's or any other way to get music into the
room, into your soul. As you play, you can dance, clap
your hands, grab two pot lids and clang them together.

Go wild.

Let yourself loose and praise the LORD!

6

Review The Doors, Your Steps To Success

Let's review: THERE ARE THREE DOORS YOU NEED TO GO THROUGH if you want to bring healing to your anxiety.

Door 1 - Getting Unstuck. Here you move off the chair of anxiety, out of the darkness into the light. You discover that you were making yourself anxious by the way you interpreted various events that happened to you. You learned that if you changed your INTERPRETATIONS, you could change how you felt. You tried it, and it works!

You then went on and changed your actions - breathing, standing up straight, going for a walk, smiling, even laughing. These actions helped your brain to accept the new interpretations you were making about the negative events that happened to you.

Door 2 - God's LOVE. You saw that all your thoughts flowed from foundational beliefs, and the greatest foundational belief is God's LOVE FOR **YOU**. You don't have to earn it. He loves you no matter what you have ever done. He can't help it, because he is pure, personal love. When you embrace his love it will change everything.

Door 3 - Opening your SOUL to God. This is where the real healing takes place. God wants to breathe his life into your soul, and when he does, you experience a healing to the depth that is unimaginable. His life becomes yours. There is that unusual exchange where you share each other's lives.

It's a miracle!

Impossible? Not at all. In fact it is promised by God himself and has been experienced by millions of people over the years.

Abby walked through all three doors. And now, today, her life is full and fulfilled. There is a depth of satisfaction that nothing else ever brought her.

And now those doors is open for you.

Walk through them.

Allow the life of God to penetrate the center of your existence.

And enjoy a life that is like Abby's…

FULL AND FULFILLED
WITH AN
INNER
SATISFACTION
THAT
NEVER ENDS.

A Prayer For You To Pray…Now

Dear LORD GOD
My FATHER
My Creator
My Hope.
You proved your love for me
Through your Son, Jesus Christ
And now it is your desire to restore my soul.
I come to you with my anxiety
To find new hope and joy in YOU.
I let you into my soul
Fully
Without reservation
Drinking in your presence
Trusting YOU to restore it.
Thank you for your
Healing power
And for the new joy you will bring.
Amen

FREE BOOKS
For
YOU!

Be sure and go to <u>DrPaulYoung.com</u> and sign up for a **free book**, a book designed to take you to a new level in your walk with God.

And keep watching this site because new free books will be offered periodically.

Last, **pray for our ministry**. We are seeking to change the hearts and souls of thousands of people around the world and need your prayers. Send me a note at <u>pauljyoung@mac.com</u> if you will pray for us.

Thanks, and God bless you!

True Stories

If you want true stories of people and how I helped them through their depression and the exciting breakthroughs they made, see my **Dr. Paul's TOTAL Relief** series on my website at <u>DrPaulYoung.com</u>.

This series also has very helpful workbooks and **"YES!" Cards** that will help you change your thoughts and actions so that you can break out of your depression and anxiety.

You can even download these "YES!" Cards to go along with what you learned in this book. The three books of cards fit right into the three doors you went through. Take a look at them. It may be just the medicine you need for your soul.

It's magical!

Or you might want to read a most unusual book, *Potato Salad For The Depressed Soul.* This is one of those books that will catch you by surprise - the way it will revamp your thinking as you make potato salad.

There is also a book in the Bible that has "JOY" in it more than any other, the book of Philippians. I took this book and personalized it, writing as if it was written to YOU. It has helped many people who are struggling with anxiety and depression to find hope and joy again. You can download it to your phone or other device and carry this wonderful message from God, personally to you. It's called: *The Personalized Bible - Philippians.* Go to DrPaulYoung.com

I have another book written to those who lost so much through the fires that swept through Santa Rosa, California with over 5,000 homes burned to the ground in just a couple hours.

We were chased out of our home for 13 days - frightened, anxious and all that one experiences during a time of horrific destruction. The book's name is *Guaranteed Recovery* After a Loss.

You may have lost a mate, gone through a divorce, lost a lot of money or a personal friend who will no longer see you. So much loss. How do you deal with it? This book will help. It's short yet powerful. Again, you can find it on DrPaulYoung.com

My most unusual book, **Dr. Paul's FEELING GOOD ToolKit** has hundreds of charts that will help you reinterpret any event and add actions that will break the back of depression and anxiety.

I write books that help, are practical, not theoretical with contents that have been proven to release people from anxiety.

Download other Dr. Paul's 99¢ Cures

Dr. Paul J. Young

Education:

University of California, Fresno, B.A in English

Dallas Theological Seminary, Th.M (Masters in Theology)

Biola University, Doctorate of Ministry with emphasis on psychology (working with Talbot School of Theology, Rosemead School of Psychology and other schools)

Dr. Paul Joseph Young

Dr. Young helped grow one of the largest churches in the Dallas/Ft. Worth area as its pastor, working with thousands of people, developing his skills both as a minister, communicator and a counselor, working with hundreds of people and developing his unique therapy techniques.

For seven years he was C.E.O. of Community Bible Study International, working in over 60 countries of the world, sharing his message of hope and joy. He held seminars on anxiety, anxiety, stress, fear, anger, and a host of other topics, seeking to bring healing to the thousands in need.

Dr. Paul's communication skills has made him a favorite speaker around the world. He lives with his wife and best friend, Diane. They have five children and 14 grandchildren.

More than anything, Dr. Paul lives to help people find the joyful, peaceful life they deserve.

This is a

DrPaulYoung.com

Publication

____